CONTENTS

COME THOU FOUNT, COME THOU KING

Traditional
Additional Words and Music by THOMAS MILLER
Arranged by Heather Sorenson

Relaxed motion (♩ = 128)

With pedal

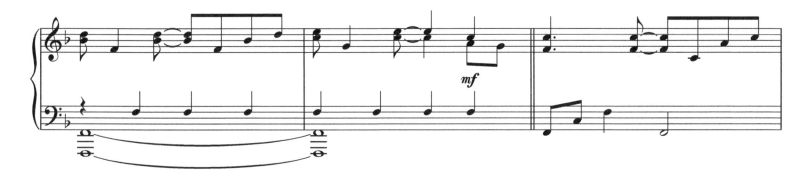

bring out melody

Expressive, rubato (♩ = 86)

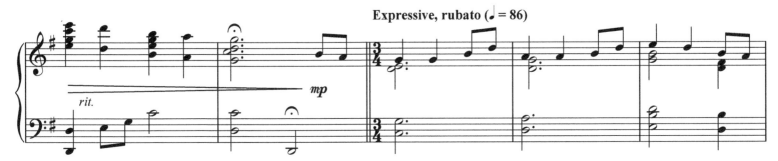

GOD OF HEAVEN

Words and Music by
HEATHER SORENSON

Ethereal (♩ = 102)

With pedal

Broadly (♩ = 92)

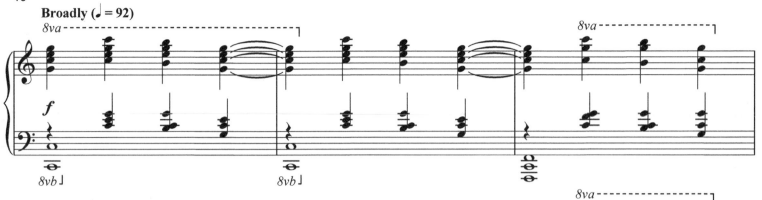

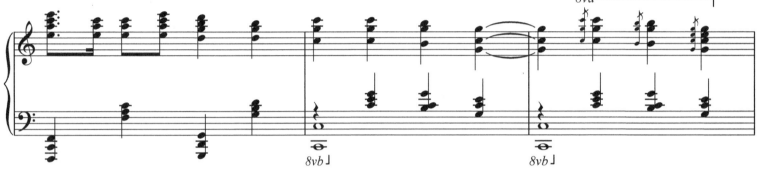

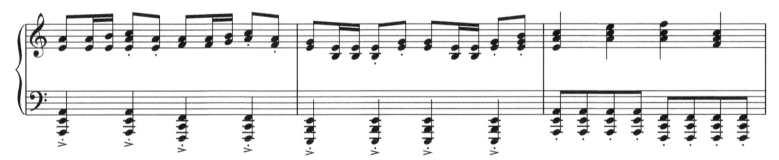

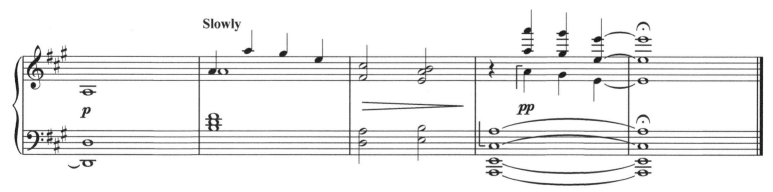

HOLY IS THE LORD
(with "Holy, Holy, Holy")

Words and Music by CHRIS TOMLIN
and LOUIE GIGLIO
Arranged by Heather Sorenson

With high energy (♩ = 128)

With pedal

Rhythmic

HOLY, HOLY, HOLY

Text by REGINALD HEBER
Music by JOHN B. DYKES

HOLY SPIRIT

Words and Music by KATIE TORWALT
and BRYAN TORWALT
Arranged by Heather Sorenson

Slower (♩ = 64)

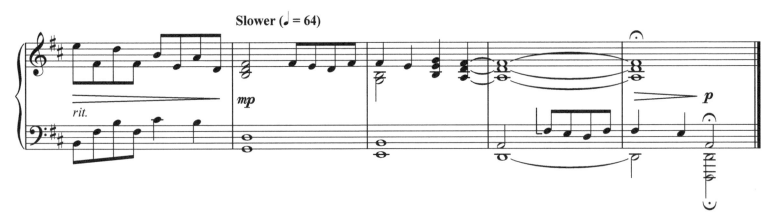

REVELATION SONG

Words and Music by
JENNIE LEE RIDDLE
Arranged by Heather Sorenson

Ethereal (♩ = 66)

p legato

With pedal

poco rit.

bring out melody

mp a tempo

Tempo I (♩ = 60)

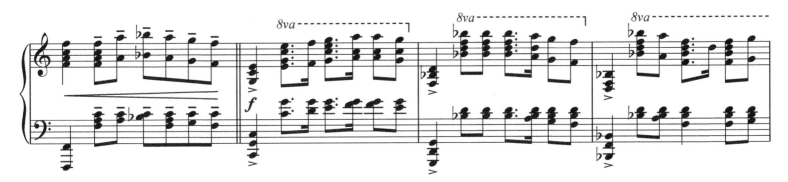

I WILL RISE

Words and Music by CHRIS TOMLIN, JESSE REEVES,
LOUIE GIGLIO and MATT MAHER
Arranged by Heather Sorenson

With feeling (♩ = 84)

With pedal

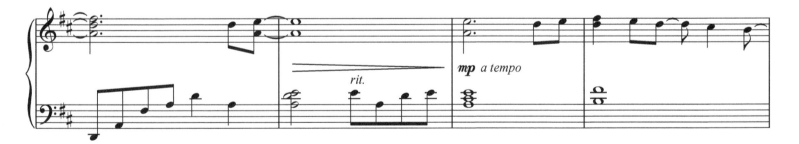

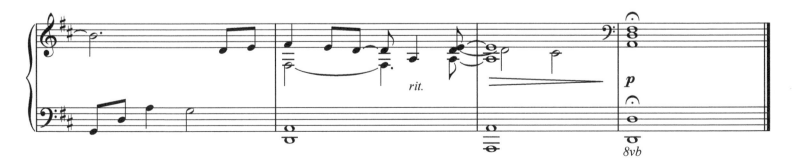

IN CHRIST ALONE

Words and Music by KEITH GETTY
and STUART TOWNEND
Arranged by Heather Sorenson

Light Classical ($\quarternote$ = 86)

Majestic (♩ = 78)

Tempo I (♩ = 86)

RAISE YOUR HANDS

Words and Music by
HEATHER SORENSON

Expressive (♩ = 106)

With pedal

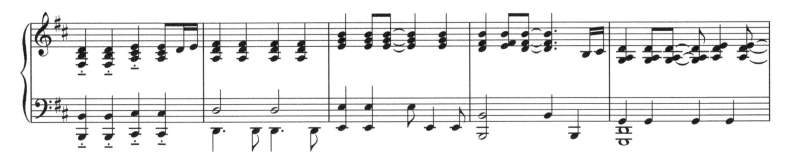

10,000 REASONS
(Bless the Lord)

Words and Music by JONAS MYRIN
and MATT REDMAN
Arranged by Heather Sorenson

With feeling (♩ = 78)

Slightly faster (♩ = 84)

Slower, rubato (♩ = 72)

Broadly (♩ = 78)

YOUR NAME
(with "All Hail the Power of Jesus' Name")

Words and Music by PAUL BALOCHE
and GLENN PACKIAM
Arranged by Heather Sorenson

ALL HAIL THE POWER OF JESUS' NAME
Words by EDWARD PERRONET
Altered by JOHN RIPPON
Music by OLIVER HOLDEN

The Best
PRAISE & WORSHIP
Songbooks for Piano

Above All
THE PHILLIP KEVEREN SERIES
15 beautiful praise song piano solo arrangements by Phillip Keveren. Includes: Above All • Agnus Dei • Breathe • Draw Me Close • He Is Exalted • I Stand in Awe • Step by Step • We Fall Down • You Are My King (Amazing Love) • and more.
00311024 Piano Solo...................................$12.99

Blended Worship Piano Collection
Songs include: Amazing Grace (My Chains Are Gone) • Be Thou My Vision • Cornerstone • Fairest Lord Jesus • Great Is Thy Faithfulness • How Great Is Our God • I Will Rise • Joyful, Joyful, We Adore Thee • Lamb of God • Majesty • Open the Eyes of My Heart • Praise to the Lord, the Almighty • Shout to the Lord • 10,000 Reasons (Bless the Lord) • Worthy Is the Lamb • Your Name • and more.
00293528 Piano Solo $17.99

Blessings
THE PHILLIP KEVEREN SERIES
Phillip Keveren delivers another stellar collection of piano solo arrangements perfect for any reverent or worship setting: Blessed Be Your Name • Blessings • Cornerstone • Holy Spirit • This Is Amazing Grace • We Believe • Your Great Name • Your Name • and more.
00156601 Piano Solo $12.99

The Best Praise & Worship Songs Ever
80 all-time favorites: Awesome God • Breathe • Days of Elijah • Here I Am to Worship • I Could Sing of Your Love Forever • Open the Eyes of My Heart • Shout to the Lord • We Bow Down • dozens more.
00311057 P/V/G...$22.99

The Big Book of Praise & Worship
Over 50 worship favorites are presented in this popular "Big Book" series collection. Includes: Always • Cornerstone • Forever Reign • I Will Follow • Jesus Paid It All • Lord, I Need You • Mighty to Save • Our God • Stronger • 10,000 Reasons (Bless the Lord) • This Is Amazing Grace • and more.
00140795 P/V/G $24.99

Contemporary Worship Duets
arr. Bill Wolaver
Contains 8 powerful songs carefully arranged by Bill Wolaver as duets for intermediate-level players: Agnus Dei • Be unto Your Name • He Is Exalted • Here I Am to Worship • I Will Rise • The Potter's Hand • Revelation Song • Your Name.
00290593 Piano Duets $10.99

The Best of Passion
Over 40 worship favorites featuring the talents of David Crowder, Matt Redman, Chris Tomlin, and others. Songs include: Always • Awakening • Blessed Be Your Name • Jesus Paid It All • My Heart Is Yours • Our God • 10,000 Reasons (Bless the Lord) • and more.
00101888 P/V/G $19.99

HAL•LEONARD®
www.halleonard.com
P/V/G = Piano/Vocal/Guitar Arrangements

Prices, contents, and availability subject to change without notice.

Praise & Worship Duets
THE PHILLIP KEVEREN SERIES
8 worshipful duets by Phillip Keveren: As the Deer • Awesome God • Give Thanks • Great Is the Lord • Lord, I Lift Your Name on High • Shout to the Lord • There Is a Redeemer • We Fall Down.
00311203 Piano Duet................................$12.99

Shout to the Lord!
THE PHILLIP KEVEREN SERIES
14 favorite praise songs, including: As the Deer • El Shaddai • Give Thanks • Great Is the Lord • How Beautiful • More Precious Than Silver • Oh Lord, You're Beautiful • A Shield About Me • Shine, Jesus, Shine • Shout to the Lord • Thy Word • and more.
00310699 Piano Solo $14.99

Sunday Solos in the Key of C
CLASSIC & CONTEMPORARY WORSHIP SONGS
22 C-major selections, including: Above All • Good Good Father • His Name Is Wonderful • Holy Spirit • Lord, I Need You • Reckless Love • What a Beautiful Name • You Are My All in All • and more.
00301044 Piano Solo $14.99

The Chris Tomlin Collection – 2nd Edition
15 songs from one of the leading artists and composers in Contemporary Christian music, including the favorites: Amazing Grace (My Chains Are Gone) • Holy Is the Lord • How Can I Keep from Singing • How Great Is Our God • Jesus Messiah • Our God • We Fall Down • and more.
00306951 P/V/G $17.99

Top Christian Downloads
21 of Christian music's top hits are presented in this collection of intermediate level piano solo arrangements. Includes: Forever Reign • How Great Is Our God • Mighty to Save • Praise You in This Storm • 10,000 Reasons (Bless the Lord) • Your Grace Is Enough • and more.
00125051 Piano Solo.................................$14.99

Top 25 Worship Songs
25 contemporary worship hits includes: Glorious Day (Passion) • Good, Good Father (Chris Tomlin) • Holy Spirit (Francesca Battistelli) • King of My Heart (John Mark & Sarah McMillan) • The Lion and the Lamb (Big Daddy Weave) • Reckless Love (Cory Asbury) • 10,000 Reasons (Matt Redman) • This Is Amazing Grace (Phil Wickham) • What a Beautiful Name (Hillsong Worship) • and more.
00288610 P/V/G $17.99

Top Worship Downloads
20 of today's chart-topping Christian hits, including: Cornerstone • Forever Reign • Great I Am • Here for You • Lord, I Need You • My God • Never Once • One Thing Remains (Your Love Never Fails) • Your Great Name • and more.
00120870 P/V/G $16.99

The World's Greatest Praise Songs
Shawnee Press
This is a unique and useful collection of 50 of the very best praise titles of the last three decades. Includes: Above All • Forever • Here I Am to Worship • I Could Sing of Your Love Forever • Open the Eyes of My Heart • and so many more.
35022891 P/V/G $19.99